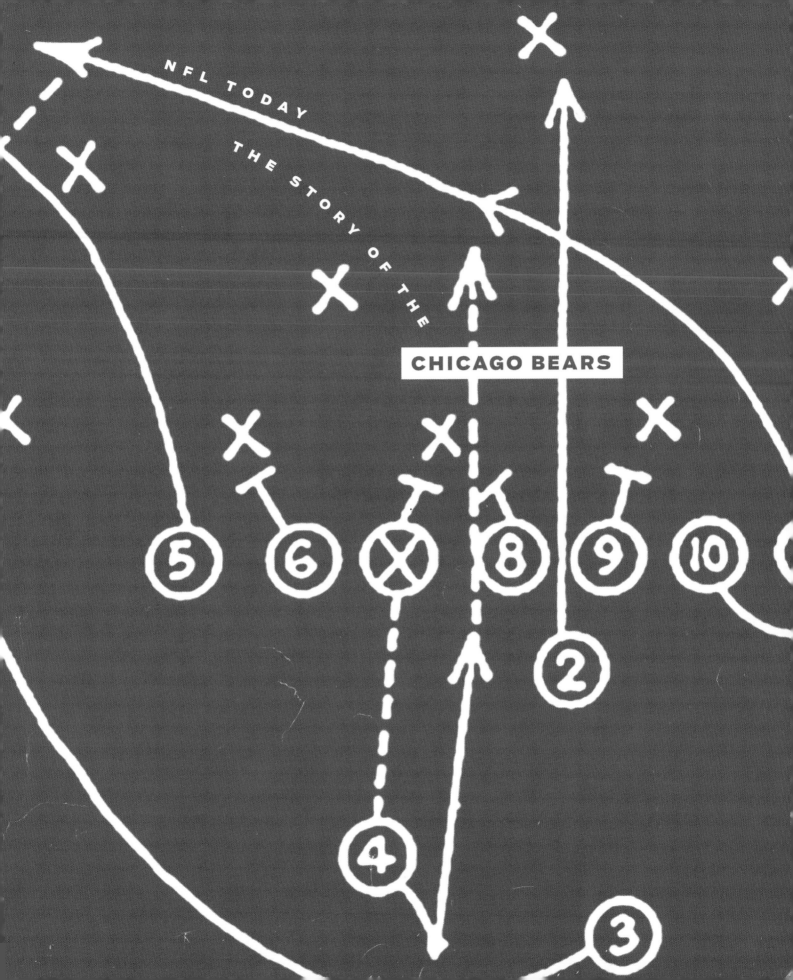

NFL TODAY

THE STORY OF THE

CHICAGO BEARS

THE STORY OF THE CHICAGO BEARS

JIM WHITING

CREATIVE EDUCATION

PUBLISHED BY CREATIVE EDUCATION
P.O. BOX 227, MANKATO, MINNESOTA 56002
CREATIVE EDUCATION IS AN IMPRINT OF THE CREATIVE COMPANY
WWW.THECREATIVECOMPANY.US

DESIGN AND PRODUCTION BY BLUE DESIGN
ART DIRECTION BY RITA MARSHALL
PRINTED IN THE UNITED STATES OF AMERICA

PHOTOGRAPHS BY ALAMY (DAVID BALL), AP
IMAGES, GETTY IMAGES (LEE BALTERMAN/SPORTS
ILLUSTRATED, VERNON BIEVER/NFL, SCOTT BOEHM,
SCOTT CUNNINGHAM, JONATHAN DANIEL, BILL
EPPRIDGE/TIME & LIFE PICTURES, JONATHAN FERREY,
FOCUS ON SPORT, SCOTT HALLERAN, JED JACOBSOHN,
KIDWILER COLLECTION/DIAMOND IMAGES, DON
LANSU/NFL, STREETER LECKA, AL MESSERSCHMIDT,
DONALD MIRALLE, RONALD C. MODRA/SPORTS
IMAGERY, PAUL NATKINI/NFL, NEW YORK TIMES
CO., PRO FOOTBALL HALL OF FAME/NFL, ROBERT
RIGER, VIC STEIN/NFL PHOTOS, ROB TRINGALI/
SPORTSCHROME, HERBERT WEITMAN/NFL)

LIBRARY OF CONGRESS CATALOGING-IN-PUBLICATION DATA
WHITING, JIM.
THE STORY OF THE CHICAGO BEARS / BY JIM WHITING.
P. CM. — (NFL TODAY)
INCLUDES INDEX.
SUMMARY: THE HISTORY OF THE NATIONAL FOOTBALL LEAGUE'S
CHICAGO BEARS, SURVEYING THE FRANCHISE'S BIGGEST STARS
AND MOST MEMORABLE MOMENTS FROM ITS INAUGURAL SEASON
IN 1920 TO TODAY.
ISBN 978-1-60818-297-8
1. CHICAGO BEARS (FOOTBALL TEAM)—HISTORY—JUVENILE
LITERATURE. I. TITLE.

GV956.C5W43 2013
796.332'640977311—DC23   2012027963

FIRST EDITION
9 8 7 6 5 4 3 2 1

COVER AND PAGE 2: RUNNING BACK MATT FORTE
PAGES 4–5: FULLBACK JOE MARCONI (#34)
PAGE 6: LINEBACKER BRIAN URLACHER

TABLE OF CONTENTS

SIDELINE STORIES

MEET THE BEARS

CHICAGO IS FAMED FOR ITS NUMEROUS HISTORIC SKYSCRAPERS

Papa Bear's Family

When he was trying to persuade the International Olympic Committee to select Chicago, Illinois, to host the 2016 Summer Olympics, United States president Barack Obama called it "the most American of American cities." People of all political persuasions agree with him. One was writer Carl Sandburg, whose poetry is closely associated with Chicago. In one of his most famous works, titled simply "Chicago" and dated about 1916, Sandburg writes, "Come and show me another city with lifted head singing / so proud to be alive and coarse and strong and cunning." In the same poem, he writes, "Stormy, husky, brawling / City of the Big Shoulders." That almost sounds like a description of the Chicago Bears professional football team, which came along a few years later.

The story of "Da Bears," as they are fondly called by their fans, began in Decatur, Illinois, about 150 miles southwest of Chicago. In 1920, Augustus Staley, owner of the Staley Starch Company, asked George Halas, a 25-year-old athlete and businessman,

EARLY GREAT RED GRANGE HELPED FOUND A WINNING TRADITION IN CHICAGO

George Halas

TEAM FOUNDER, OWNER, COACH / **BEARS SEASONS: 1920–83 (AS OWNER); 1920–29, 1933–41, 1946–55, 1958–67 (AS COACH)**

Born and raised on the west side of Chicago, George "Papa Bear" Halas founded, played for, coached, and owned the Chicago Bears. While studying at the University of Illinois, Halas played football, basketball, and baseball. He spent time in the U.S. Navy and played 12 games for the New York Yankees baseball team as an outfielder, then switched over to football. He founded a team called the Decatur Staleys in 1920 that would become the Chicago Bears by 1922. Halas played for the Staleys/Bears from 1920 to 1929, mostly on defense, and once returned a fumble 98 yards for a touchdown. In the 1930s, he concentrated solely on coaching, building the Bears into a powerhouse that won NFL championships in 1932, 1933, 1940, 1941, 1943, 1946, and 1963. Bears players described Halas as a taskmaster, and he was the first coach to hold daily practice sessions and analyze films of games to further his coaching strategies. Among his accomplishments was the perfecting of the T-formation (an offensive set in which three running backs lined up five yards behind the quarterback), which became all the rage in football in the 1940s.

Top Row—Dr. J. F. Davis, C. Tackwell, John Sisk, John Doehring, Bill Buckler, Paul Franklin, Tiny Engebretsen, A. Lotshaw, Ralph Jones.
Middle Row—Charles Bidwill, George Trafton, Don Murry, L. Burdick, Gil Bergerson, Bronko Nagurski, Luke Johnsos, Bert Pearson, George Halas.
Front Row—Dick Nesbitt, Bill Hewitt, Carl Brumbaugh, Keith Molesworth, Red Grange, George Corbett, Ookie Miller, Jules Carlson, Joe Kopcha.

to help form a pro football team known as the Decatur Staleys. Halas met with representatives of other budding franchises in the Midwest to form the American Professional Football Association (renamed the National Football League, or NFL, two years later).

H alas did a little bit of everything in the team's early years. He sold tickets, taped ankles, shoveled snow, coached, and played end. Thanks to his efforts and those of such players as running back Ed "Dutch" Sternaman, the Staleys were an instant success, going 9–1–1 in 1921 and winning the league championship.

A year later, the club moved to Chicago. Halas bought a controlling interest in the team and changed its name. Chicago had a baseball team named the Cubs. Halas reasoned that football players were larger than baseball players and accordingly said they would become the Bears. Halas, who would become known as "Papa Bear," would own the team for the next 62 years, acting as coach for 40 of them.

"It was like getting an electric shock."

**RED GRANGE ON HITTING
BRONKO NAGURSKI**

Halas ensured that the Bears would remain a powerhouse by signing running back Harold "Red" Grange, who had once run for 263 yards and 4 touchdowns in a single quarter in a collegiate game. His shifty running style earned him the nickname "The Galloping Ghost" and made him the most famous football player of his day—the game's premier superstar. Halas signed Grange the day after his final college game in 1925, paying him $100,000 in an era when the average player received $100 per game. Grange was the featured attraction as the Bears went on a famous 19-game, 66-day cross-country tour soon after he joined the team. Many sports historians credit this tour with making pro football legitimate in the eyes of the American public—perhaps even keeping it from folding altogether.

hicago's backfield received an upgrade in 1930 from fullback Bronislau "Bronko" Nagurski. At 6-foot-2 and 230 pounds (a size considered enormous in those days), the northern Minnesota farmboy was a punishing runner. But he was perhaps most fearsome as a blocker who paved the way for Grange. "When you hit him, it was like getting an electric shock," said Grange. "If you hit him above the ankles, you were likely to get yourself killed."

The Bears won two NFL championships in the 1930s, when Chicago featured a number of great players such as speedy running back Beattie Feathers and rough-and-tumble center George Trafton. But Grange and Nagurski were the heart of the team. The Bears won the 1932 championship when the NFL held its first-ever playoff game. The conditions were cold and windy in Chicago, so the game was

CENTER GEORGE TRAFTON

The Staley Swindle

The two best teams in football in 1921 were the Chicago Staleys and the Buffalo All-Americans. Both were undefeated before a Thanksgiving Day matchup, which Buffalo won 7–6. Chicago coach George Halas demanded a rematch. Buffalo agreed, with one condition: the game, scheduled for December 4, would be an exhibition and not count in the standings. After winning their final regular-season game on December 3—giving them a 9–0 record to Chicago's 7–1 and therefore the league title—the All-Americans took an overnight train to Chicago. Not surprisingly, the Staleys defeated the exhausted All-Americans 10–7. Sensing an opportunity, Halas quickly scheduled two more games, and the Staleys won one and tied the other. Now Halas claimed that since both teams had identical 9–1 records (ties were thrown out) and the Staleys had won the second—and more important—meeting, the title should be theirs. The league quickly passed a ruling that sided with Halas's reasoning, and the Staleys were declared the champs. Calling the outcome the "Staley Swindle," Buffalo owner Frank McNeil—who had purchased tiny gold footballs for his team as mementos of their championship before the second game with Chicago—spent the rest of his life trying to get the decision overturned.

THE STALEYS/BEARS HAD WINNING RECORDS IN 24 OF THEIR FIRST 25 SEASONS

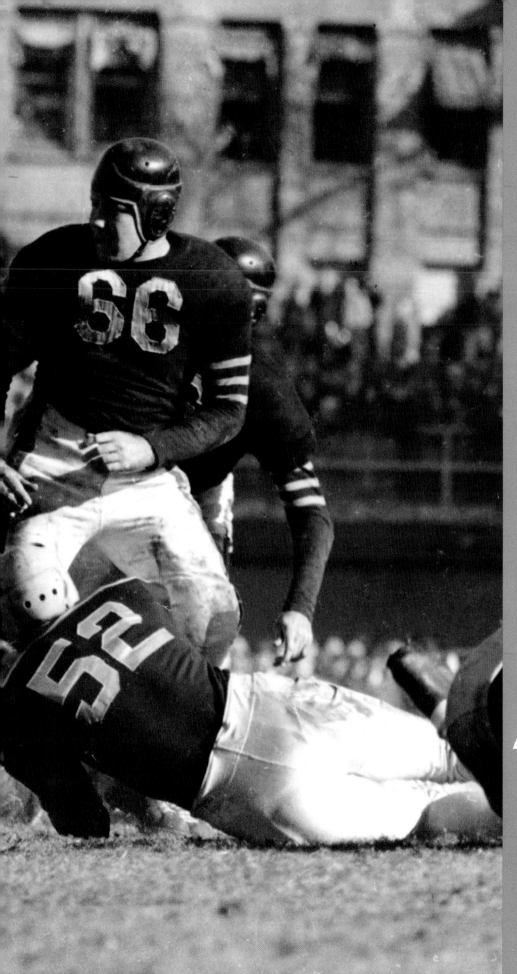

moved from Wrigley Field to inside Chicago Stadium. The Bears and their opponent, the Portsmouth Spartans, were tied at zero in the fourth quarter. Chicago scored on a controversial play when quarterback Dutch Brumbaugh handed off to Nagurski, who threw a short pass to Grange in the end zone. League rules at the time mandated that any forward pass be launched from a minimum of five yards behind the line of scrimmage, and the Spartans argued that Grange was not far enough behind the line when he passed. But the score stood, and the Bears won, 9–0.

A year later, 26,000 fans showed up at Wrigley Field to watch the Bears take on the New York Giants for the 1933 NFL championship. Nagurski's passing prowess produced two touchdowns, and the

✕ Bronko Nagurski

FULLBACK, LINEBACKER, OFFENSIVE TACKLE / BEARS SEASONS: 1930–37, 1943 / HEIGHT: 6-FOOT-2 / WEIGHT: 230 POUNDS

Bronislau "Bronko" Nagurski (right) was the most powerful football player before World War II. Born in Canada and raised in International Falls, Minnesota, Nagurski came from Polish stock. He played collegiate football at the University of Minnesota and had a sensational career there, earning All-American honors on both offense and defense. The Bears signed him in 1930 and soon reaped the benefits of his skill at running, tackling, blocking, and even passing. Often, Nagurski was simply a wrecking ball swinging straight through opposing players. Famed fullback Ernie Nevers of the Duluth Eskimos and Chicago Cardinals once said, "Tackling Bronko was like trying to stop a freight train running downhill." Nagurski helped the Bears win league championships in 1932 and 1933 and then came out of a five-year retirement to help Chicago to another title in 1943 as the Bears defeated the Washington Redskins 41–21. After his football days ended, Nagurski launched a successful career in professional wrestling. Later in life, he retired to International Falls and opened a service station, living to the age of 81.

Soldier Field

For the first 49 years of their existence, the Chicago Bears made their home at Wrigley Field. Then, in 1971, when the NFL ruled that all teams must play in stadiums with room for at least 50,000 fans, the Bears moved across town and into Soldier Field. Located only a few hundred yards west of Lake Michigan, Soldier Field had been constructed in the early 1920s as a memorial to American soldiers who had died in wars. Built to resemble great buildings of ancient Greece and Rome, Soldier Field was a versatile recreational venue that hosted championship boxing matches, rodeos, car races, circuses, and operas, among other events. In 2002 and 2003, the grand old stadium was essentially rebuilt at a cost of almost $630 million. Soldier Field's most identifiable features—its classical, 100-foot colonnades— were preserved, but they were dwarfed by a new metallic façade that raised the seating structure much higher. Although it seemed a majority of fans disliked the new, futuristic-looking exterior (many people said it looked like a flying saucer had landed on the stadium), most agreed that Soldier Field's interior was improved, offering better viewing angles.

SOLDIER FIELD IS ONE OF THE SMALLEST NFL STADIUMS IN TERMS OF SEATING CAPACITY

✕Sid Luckman

QUARTERBACK / BEARS SEASONS: 1939–50 / HEIGHT: 6 FEET / WEIGHT: 200 POUNDS

From 1940 to 1946, the Bears played in five NFL Championship Games, winning four, and Sid Luckman, the team's quarterback and triggerman on their vaunted T-formation attack, was a major reason why. In 1937 and 1938, the Brooklyn-born Luckman was named an All-American at Columbia University. He planned on leaving football behind after college, but legendary Bears coach George Halas gave Luckman a playbook featuring plays from the T-formation, and the idea intrigued Luckman enough that he signed with the Bears in 1939. In 1940, he had a breakout year as the Bears' offense clicked, and Chicago stormed to a 73–0 win in the NFL Championship Game versus the Washington Redskins. Equally adept at passing and running, Luckman was also a natural leader. After retiring as a player, he spent many years coaching, including at his alma mater, Columbia. The school tried to pay Luckman for his efforts. He refused to accept it, though, returning the money with a note saying he'd rather see it go to a "worthy student."

"...quitters and a bunch of crybabies."

REDSKINS OWNER GEORGE MARSHALL ON THE BEARS

Bears led late in the game, 23–21. On the final play, Giants receiver Dale Burnett sped downfield with a teammate trailing a few yards behind. Grange was the only Bears defender between them and the goal line. He knew that if he tackled Burnett, the receiver would lateral to his teammate, who would score the game-winning touchdown. "So I grabbed Burnett around the chest and held his arms so he couldn't lateral," Grange explained. Halas described it as "the greatest defensive play I ever saw."

By the end of the 1930s, age and injuries had caught up with The Galloping Ghost and Nagurski. Halas then found a new player who would keep Chicago flying high—Sid Luckman, a talented college running back who became a quarterback after joining the Bears in 1939. With Luckman leading the offense and lightning-fast safety George McAfee (also a star runner and kick returner) sparking the defense, the Bears—nicknamed "The Monsters of the Midway"—went a stunning 37–5–1 from 1940 to 1943.

The Bears played some outstanding games during that stretch, but no performance came as close to perfection as the 1940 NFL Championship Game against the Washington Redskins. Chicago had lost to the Redskins, 7–3, several weeks earlier. When the Bears complained about a controversial call, Redskins owner George Marshall called them "quitters and a bunch of crybabies." In the title game, playing with pride and anger, Chicago destroyed Washington 73–0 in the most lopsided NFL game of all time. It got so bad that the referees asked the Bears to stop kicking extra points. So many balls had been booted into the stands that the officials were running out of footballs. After the game, Redskins quarterback Sammy Baugh was asked if things would have been different if his receiver hadn't dropped a sure touchdown pass in the first quarter. "Sure," said Baugh. "The final score would've been 73–7."

Chicago Legends

In 1941, the Bears beat the Giants for the NFL championship. In 1942, Chicago was undefeated until the championship game, when Washington pulled off a 14–6 upset. In 1943, the Bears got their revenge, besting the Redskins in a championship rematch, 41–21.

In 1946, after a couple of subpar seasons, Chicago again knocked off the Giants for the NFL championship. But after Luckman retired in 1951, Chicago no longer dominated. As always, the team had a number of terrific players. Running back Rick Casares excited fans with his Nagurski-like rushing style, Harlon Hill became the first Bears player to post more than 1,000 receiving yards in a season, and few players were tougher or more ill-tempered than linebacker Bill George and defensive end Ed Sprinkle. Although Chicago had some moderate success from 1947 to 1962, it made the NFL title game just once, getting routed in 1956 by the Giants, 47–7.

LINEBACKER BILL GEORGE (LEFT) AND DEFENSIVE END DOUG ATKINS

A Six-Score Day

December 12, 1965, was a cold and wet day in Chicago. The Chicago Bears and San Francisco 49ers were suited up to play, and after players tested the field in pregame warm-ups, most readied themselves for what they presumed would be a grind-it-out game on the sloppy Wrigley Field turf. But on the second play of the game, Gale Sayers, a rookie Bears running back nicknamed "The Kansas Comet," caught a short screen pass and darted through the entire 49ers defense for a touchdown. In the second quarter, Sayers took a pitchout 21 yards for a score, and then followed that up with a 7-yard jaunt to pay dirt. And that was just the first half. In the second half, Sayers scored three more touchdowns for an NFL record of six in one game. The final score came on an electrifying 85-yard punt return. Sayers's performance left all those in attendance amazed. "The mud affected the kid," said Bears tight end Mike Ditka after the game. "If it had been dry out there, he would've scored 10 touchdowns."

GALE SAYERS WAS BORN IN KANSAS AND PLAYED COLLEGE FOOTBALL THERE

Sid Luckman

QUARTERBACK / BEARS SEASONS: 1939–50 / HEIGHT: 6 FEET / WEIGHT: 200 POUNDS

From 1940 to 1946, the Bears played in five NFL Championship Games, winning four, and Sid Luckman, the team's quarterback and triggerman on their vaunted T-formation attack, was a major reason why. In 1937 and 1938, the Brooklyn-born Luckman was named an All-American at Columbia University. He planned on leaving football behind after college, but legendary Bears coach George Halas gave Luckman a playbook featuring plays from the T-formation, and the idea intrigued Luckman enough that he signed with the Bears in 1939. In 1940, he had a breakout year as the Bears' offense clicked, and Chicago stormed to a 73–0 win in the NFL Championship Game versus the Washington Redskins. Equally adept at passing and running, Luckman was also a natural leader. After retiring as a player, he spent many years coaching, including at his alma mater, Columbia. The school tried to pay Luckman for his efforts. He refused to accept it, though, returning the money with a note saying he'd rather see it go to a "worthy student."

record 6 touchdowns—1 on a pass, 4 on runs, and 1 on an 85-yard punt return. Sadly, his career spanned only parts of seven seasons before being cut short by knee injuries.

While Sayers bewildered opponents, Butkus frightened them. Regarded by many as the most ferocious football player of all time, the 6-foot-3 and 245-pound linebacker played every snap with reckless abandon. Even though the Bears had a winning record only twice during his nine-year career, Butkus never stopped giving his all. "It's like he was from another world, another planet," Miami Dolphins guard Bob Kuechenberg later marveled. "He didn't run a [fast 40-yard dash], he wasn't a great weight lifter, but he just ate them alive, all those … sprinters and 500-pound bench pressers."

When Butkus retired after the 1973 season, fans had to wait only a single year for the next Bears legend to emerge: Walter Payton, a running back who, as a kid, had been more interested in band and gymnastics than football. Although Payton weighed just 200 pounds and was nicknamed "Sweetness," he was a classic Bears rusher who enjoyed running over—not around—defenders. Amazingly, despite his hard-nosed running style, he would miss only 1 game in his 13-year career.

From 1976 to 1986, Payton rushed for more than 1,000 yards every season except in 1982 (when a players' strike broke the streak). Before his playing days ended, Sweetness would carry the ball more times (3,838) for more yards (16,726) than any other player in NFL history. Perhaps the most remarkable thing was that he did it despite the mediocre talent in Chicago during most of those years. As former San Diego Chargers tight end Kellen Winslow noted, "For most of his career, he took on the NFL with no offensive line."

Brian's Song

Brian Piccolo joined the Bears in 1966, one year after Gale Sayers, and the two shared a common position at running back and a similar zest for life. Unfortunately, late in the 1969 season, a large, cancerous tumor was found in Piccolo's left lung. During Piccolo's struggles with cancer and recuperations from surgeries, Sayers had knee surgery, which required long bouts of rehabilitation. The two players encouraged each other through their respective hardships. While Sayers eventually recovered, Piccolo did not and died on June 16, 1970, at age 26. Sayers was so moved by Piccolo's courage that he wrote a memoir largely about his friendship with Piccolo, which became the basis for a made-for-television movie called *Brian's Song*. In addition to being a poignant story about friendship, life, death, and football, the movie had an unexpected effect on viewers. At a time when America was wrestling with race riots and race discrimination, the movie, about a black man and a white man befriending and helping one another, offered an intelligent look at the fulfillment that could come from such supportive and unprejudiced relationships.

BRIAN PICCOLO RAN FOR ALMOST 1,000 YARDS IN 4 CHICAGO SEASONS

JIM McMAHON WAS A LEADER KNOWN FOR HIS POISE IN THE POCKET

A Team for the Ages

In 1982, 87-year-old George Halas, who still owned the team, put the Bears in the hands of a new coach: former star end Mike Ditka. "Iron Mike" had earned a reputation as a tough guy during his playing days in the 1960s, and the fiery coach soon had the team on the rise. Behind the great play of Payton, quarterback Jim McMahon, safety Gary Fencik, defensive end Dan Hampton, and linebacker Mike Singletary, the Bears went 8–8 in 1983 and 10–6 in 1984.

By 1985, the Bears were poised for greatness. Payton was still explosive, and Chicago's defense—molded by feisty defensive coordinator Buddy Ryan—was the NFL's best. The Bears won their first 12 games in 1985 and finished with a 15–1 record. Defensive end Richard Dent led the NFL with 17 quarterback sacks, and the hard-hitting Singletary was named the league's Defensive Player of the Year.

In the playoffs, the Bears were unstoppable. They crushed the Giants 21–0 and the Los Angeles Rams 24–0 to reach Super Bowl XX, where they destroyed the New England Patriots 46–10 to capture the franchise's ninth league championship. "We've

WALTER PAYTON EARNED BOTH A SUPER BOWL RING AND LEGENDARY STATUS

THE SWARMING BEARS DEFENSE OVERWHELMED THE PATRIOTS IN SUPER BOWL XX

Dick Butkus

LINEBACKER / BEARS SEASONS: 1965–73 / HEIGHT: 6-FOOT-3 / WEIGHT: 245 POUNDS

With a mean streak a mile wide and the ability to intimidate even the toughest ballcarriers, Dick Butkus cut an imposing figure on the football field for the Bears. Butkus grew up on the south side of Chicago and was a two-time All-American at the University of Illinois. He joined the Bears in 1965 along with another impressive Bears rookie, running back Gale Sayers. Playing a tough sport, manning a tough position, often wearing a tough-looking mustache, and even having a tough-sounding name, Butkus quickly became a fan favorite. "When I went out on the field to warm up, I would manufacture things to make me mad," he once said to explain his on-field fierceness. "If someone on the other team was laughing, I'd pretend he was laughing at me or the Bears. It always worked for me." After a serious knee injury cut his stellar playing career short, he went on to some success as a television and commercial actor and announcer. As a tribute to his legendary defensive skills, the Dick Butkus Award is handed out yearly to college football's top linebacker.

been working hard the last two years to be the best [defense] ever," said Dent after the victory. "I believe we're in the running. If we're not, I'd like to see who's better."

Chicago continued to dominate the National Football Conference (NFC) Central Division. Between 1984 and 1988, the Bears won 62 games—at that time the most ever by any NFL team in a 5-year span. They remained powerful through 1991 with the help of such additions as running back Neal Anderson (who replaced the retired Payton). Unfortunately, the Bears could not make it back to the Super Bowl. In 1992, after Chicago went just 5–11, Ditka stepped down as head coach.

With Ditka and most of the stars of the 1980s gone, Chicago was mediocre for the rest of the '90s. Dave Wannstedt was hired as Chicago's new head coach in 1993, and Bears fans shared brief optimism when the team went 9–7 in 1994 and won an opening-round playoff game against the Minnesota Vikings. But the Bears would not make the postseason again in Wannstedt's tenure, which lasted

The Super Bowl Shuffle

Although the 1985 Chicago Bears weren't the first NFL team to sing and dance to a rally song, "The Super Bowl Shuffle" is probably the best-remembered and most widely known such song. Before the Bears' appearance in Super Bowl XX, numerous members of the team, including running back Walter Payton, quarterback Jim McMahon, linebacker Mike Singletary, receiver Willie Gault, defensive end Richard Dent, and defensive lineman William "The Refrigerator" Perry, got together to sing and dance to a rap song that was the brainchild of Gault and record producer Randy Weigand. Players took turns rapping and singing the chorus, "We ain't here to start no trouble, we're just here to do the Super Bowl Shuffle!" The song and resulting music video were smash hits when they reached airwaves and television. "The Super Bowl Shuffle" reached #41 on the Billboard Charts and #75 on the Hot R&B/Hip-Hop Chart. It was also nominated for a Grammy Award in the Best Rhythm and Blues Vocal Performance category. Some profits for the song went to charity, quelling some of the criticism the team received for being "cocky."

"THE SUPER BOWL SHUFFLE" FEATURED CHOREOGRAPHED DANCE MOVES.

HARD-HITTING SAFETY MIKE BROWN EARNED ALL-PRO HONORS IN 2001

through 1998. Bad luck abounded during those years, as several promising young players had short careers due to injuries or disappointing play after the Bears had spent high draft picks to acquire them.

In 2000, with head coach Dick Jauron at the helm, the Bears finally added the star they so desperately needed: linebacker Brian Urlacher. At 6-foot-4 and 260 pounds, Urlacher's size and skill (not to mention his crew-cut hairstyle) had people comparing him to the great Butkus. In his first NFL season, Urlacher lived up to the hype by making 165 tackles and earning Defensive Rookie of the Year honors. "It seems like he gets to places faster than anyone else," marveled Bears safety Mike Brown, also a rookie in 2000. "I've never seen someone so fast on the football field."

In 2001, the Bears ended their streak of losing football by putting together a surprising 13–3 record. Led by an aggressive defense headed by Urlacher and Brown, the Bears kept fans on the edges of their seats week after week, winning games with frantic comebacks and trick plays. In back-to-back midseason games, the scrappy Bears came back late from 15 points down to the San Francisco 49ers and 14 points down to the Cleveland Browns to win both games in overtime on interception returns by Brown. After getting a bye in the first round of the playoffs, the Bears drew the Philadelphia Eagles in the second round and briefly led 7–6 before the Eagles took control and won, 33–19.

BRIAN URLACHER ADDED TO CHICAGO'S HISTORY OF EXTRAORDINARY LINEBACKERS

LOVIE SMITH WAS KNOWN AS A SOFT-SPOKEN BUT DETERMINED LEADER

Lovie's Monsters

The next two seasons were rife with injury and underachievement as Chicago went 4–12 and 7–9. Jauron was fired, with former St. Louis Rams defensive coordinator Lovie Smith replacing him. Right away, Smith pointed to three clear goals he wanted to attain: end the decade of dominance that the longtime rival Green Bay Packers had held over the Bears, control the newly formed NFC North Division, and win the Super Bowl.

Smith's first season in Chicago, 2004, was far from exceptional, as the Bears lost quarterback Rex Grossman to a season-ending injury in the third game and shuffled through three other quarterbacks the rest of the year en route to a 5–11 mark. Still, the defense was fast improving, thanks to players such as Urlacher, cornerback Nathan Vasher, and defensive tackle Tommie Harris.

The 2005 Bears got it together for their new coach, going 11–5. Although Grossman again was lost to injury for most of the season, the Bears' defense was one of the

COACH SMITH COULD COUNT ON THE SPEED OF KICK RETURNER DEVIN HESTER

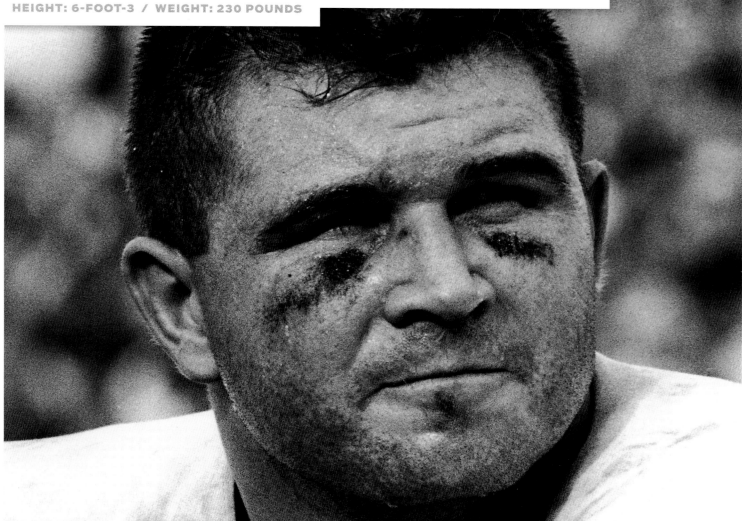

Mike Ditka

TIGHT END, COACH / BEARS SEASONS: 1961–66 (AS PLAYER), 1982–92 (AS COACH) / HEIGHT: 6-FOOT-3 / WEIGHT: 230 POUNDS

Selected by the Bears with the fifth overall pick in the 1961 NFL Draft, Mike Ditka went on to enjoy an extraordinary first season in which he caught 56 passes for 1,076 yards and 12 touchdowns and won league Rookie of the Year honors. Ditka had the sheer size to throw crushing blocks and the agility and sure hands to catch passes, and he helped increase the value that teams placed on the tight end position. He also became the first tight end to be voted into the Pro Football Hall of Fame. Bears Hall of Fame linebacker Bill George said, "Ten more like him and there would be no room for me on the team." After his playing career, Ditka turned to coaching, and the tenacity and ferocity he possessed as a player served him well on the sidelines. Some fans consider his 1985 Bears team that won Super Bowl XX to be the best team of all time. "There's more to winning than just wanting to," he once said. "You have to prove yourself every Sunday. Just throwing your helmet on the field doesn't scare anyone."

best in the league, with five members heading to the Pro Bowl after the season. Although Chicago lost its first-round playoff game 29–21 to the Carolina Panthers, Coach Smith was universally praised for turning the Bears around, garnering NFL Coach of the Year honors.

With Grossman finally healthy and running back Thomas Jones coming off a 1,335-yard rushing season, the offense of the 2006 Bears began operating at full speed and with a balanced attack. Adding to the team's offensive firepower was rookie return man Devin Hester, who ran three punts and two kickoffs back for touchdowns using his uncanny ability to weave through the sea of players speeding at him on special teams. The Bears finished the regular season an NFC-best 13–3 and earned home-field advantage throughout the playoffs.

THE 2006 BEARS CLAWED TO WITHIN ONE WIN OF A WORLD TITLE

First up were the Seattle Seahawks, with the Bears pulling out a 27–24 win on a field goal in overtime. A week later, Chicago secured a place in the Super Bowl with a 39–14 trouncing of the New Orleans Saints. Super Bowl XLI featured the strong passing attack of the Indianapolis Colts, led by quarterback Peyton Manning, versus the tough Bears defense. Hester immediately sparked Chicago when he took the game's opening kickoff 92 yards for a touchdown. Manning steadied the Colts, though, and Indianapolis pulled out the victory, 29–17. "We just never really established any kind of rhythm, running or throwing it, until it was too late," Grossman said.

hicago's 2007 campaign was marred by a slew of injuries, bad play, and missed opportunities that resulted in a 7–9 record. Hester was one of the few highlights, setting an NFL record with six punt or kickoff returns for touchdowns and forcing many teams to kick the ball away from him. To avoid "The Windy City Flyer," Detroit coach Rod Marinelli told his punter to "kick the ball into Lake Michigan and make sure it sinks to the bottom."

Many experts had low expectations for Chicago heading into the 2008 season. Once again, the Bears defied expectations, staying in the NFC North hunt with a 9–7 record, thanks to the efforts of the always tough defense and surprisingly strong play by quarterback Kyle Orton and rookie running back Matt Forte.

Prime-Time Return Man

Super Bowl XLI pitted the Bears against the Indianapolis Colts. With the rock song "Welcome to the Jungle" wafting through the stadium's speakers for the game's opening kickoff, rookie Chicago kick returner Devin Hester settled under the ball near the left sideline at the eight-yard line. Hester veered right, heading up the field. He hesitated for just an instant, faking left before continuing to the right, then put on a blazing burst of speed to get around the Colts' coverage team. Seconds later, Hester coasted into the end zone, becoming the first player in Super Bowl history to return the opening kickoff for a touchdown. "That gave us a big lift right away," said Chicago coach Lovie Smith. "Whenever you can start a game off like that, it gives you a lot of momentum." Although the momentum wouldn't last—the Bears lost 29–17—Hester's return was a moment Chicago fans would never forget. It was also a sign of things to come. Early in the 2011 season, Hester returned his 11th career punt for a touchdown, setting a new NFL record. His combined 17 (as of 2012) kickoff and punt return touchdowns are also an NFL standard.

IN COLLEGE, DEVIN HESTER PLAYED AS A CORNERBACK, RECEIVER, AND RETURNER.

THE BEARS CONSISTENTLY RANKED AMONG THE NFL'S TOP DEFENSES IN THE 2000s

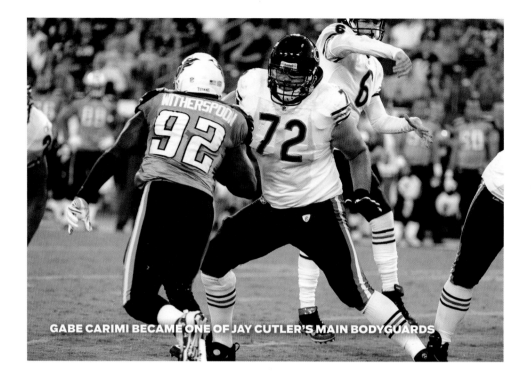

GABE CARIMI BECAME ONE OF JAY CUTLER'S MAIN BODYGUARDS

The Bears made a major shakeup by sending Orton and several draft choices to Denver in exchange for Jay Cutler, a quarterback known for his powerful arm, before the 2009 season. Although the Bears knocked off the defending Super Bowl champion Pittsburgh Steelers in Week 2, they sputtered to a 7–9 overall record.

In 2010, Cutler and the Bears roared to an 11–5 record and knocked off Seattle in the first round of the playoffs. Then, with only a home-field win standing between them and the Super Bowl, they dropped a 21–14 decision to the hated Packers in the NFC Championship Game as Cutler was sidelined in the second half by a knee injury.

With the offensive line a concern in recent seasons, the team sought to address the issue through the 2010 and 2011 Drafts by obtaining tackles J'Marcus Webb and Gabe Carimi. The moves seemed to help, as the Bears tore to a 7–3 start in 2011. But Cutler then suffered a broken thumb, and Chicago lost five games in a row to fall out of playoff contention and finish with an 8–8 mark.

Confident that another Super Bowl run was within reach, Chicago added to its offensive firepower in the off-season by trading for huge receiver Brandon Marshall, who had just been named the Most Valuable Player of the 2012 Pro Bowl. Cutler was especially excited, as the move reunited him with his favorite target when both played for Denver. "Told you we could get that #15 [Marshall's number] out of

Walter Payton

RUNNING BACK / BEARS SEASONS: 1975–87 / HEIGHT: 5-FOOT-10 / WEIGHT: 200 POUNDS

Walter Payton, a man nicknamed "Sweetness," is considered by many to be the best all-around running back the NFL has ever seen. As a youngster, Payton enjoyed music and dancing and was once a national dance competition finalist on the television show *Soul Train*. He followed his older brother Eddie, who played five seasons in the NFL, to little-known Jackson State University in Mississippi. The Bears drafted Payton in 1975 and watched him rack up rushing yards and touchdowns in bunches. With elusive moves, a sprinter's speed, durable toughness, and high-stepping style, Payton was the complete package of rushing talent. When the Bears finally built a strong offense and defense around him, they became a powerhouse and, in 1985, Super Bowl champions. Payton retired after the 1987 season yet remained a high-profile celebrity, often appearing at charity events. Sweetness missed just a single game in his entire career because of injury, an impressive feat for a running back. Sadly, his health post-football was more fragile, and he died of a rare liver disease at the age of 45.

A BIG PLAY WAS ALWAYS POSSIBLE WHEN JAY CUTLER DROPPED BACK TO PASS

JULIUS PEPPERS BROUGHT STEADY PRESSURE ON OPPOSING QUARTERBACKS

storage," Cutler told Bears fans via Twitter. "Getting the band back together!"

For the first half of the 2012 season, it looked as though the band was indeed back together. The Bears compiled a gaudy 7–1 record, capped by a 50–21 thrashing of the Tennessee Titans that included a team record of four touchdowns in the first quarter. Their point differential of 120 during that streak was the league's best. However, Chicago soon lost its luster and won only three more games. In particularly demoralizing losses to the playoff-bound Houston Texans and San Francisco 49ers in Weeks 10 and 11, the Bears managed to score a total of two field goals and a single touchdown. Although Marshall established new Bears records for receptions (118) and receiving yards (1,508) in a season, the team lost out on a playoff berth to the identically ranked Minnesota Vikings.

His consistent failure to reach the playoffs cost Coach Smith his job. As his replacement, Chicago brass tapped Marc Trestman, whose Montreal Alouettes had won the Grey Cup (Canada's equivalent of the Super Bowl) in 2010 and 2011. Trestman's expertise in working with quarterbacks gave Bears fans hope that he and Cutler would achieve a winning chemistry in the seasons to come.

From George Halas to Walter Payton to Devin Hester, the Chicago Bears can lay claim to some of the most important and exciting names in the history of pro football. Da Bears have also won more games than any other NFL franchise in their long and colorful history, and with each new season, Chicago's beloved team takes its best shot at claiming world championship number 10. When that next Super Bowl Sunday comes, the roar of the Monsters of the Midway is sure to be heard all around the sports world once again.

INDEX